ORCHIDELIRIUM

ORCHIDELIRIUM

DAVE CARLEY

Orchidelirium
first published 2004 by
Scirocco Drama
An imprint of J. Gordon Shillingford Publishing Inc.

Scirocco Drama Series Editor: Glenda MacFarlane
Cover art by Elliott Smith
Cover design by Doowah Design Inc.
Author photo by Michael Lee
Printed and bound in Canada

We acknowledge the financial support of the Manitoba Arts Council, The Canada Council for the Arts and the Government of Canada through the Book Publishing Industry Development Program (BPIDP) for our publishing program.

Production enquiries should be addressed to:
Pam Winter
Gary Goddard Agency
10 St. Mary Street, Suite 305
Toronto, Ontario, M4Y 1P9
(416) 928-1299
goddard@canadafilm.com

Canadian Cataloguing in Publication Data

Carley, Dave, 1955–
Orchidelirium/Dave Carley.

A play.
ISBN 0-920486-79-7

I. Title.

PS8555.A7397O73 2004 C812′.54 C2004-904918-6

J. Gordon Shillingford Publishing
P.O. Box 86, RPO Corydon Avenue, Winnipeg, MB Canada R3M 3S3

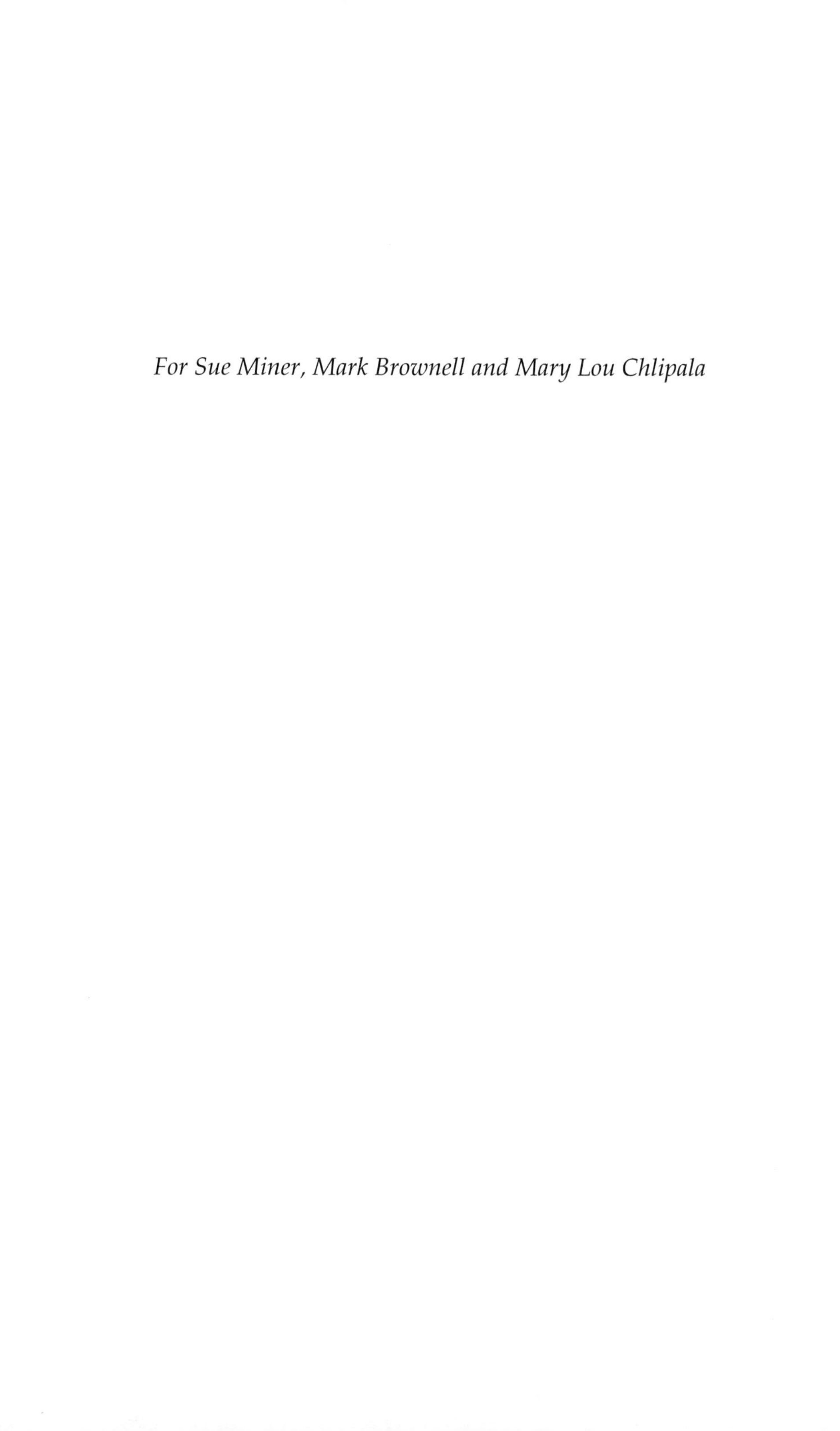

For Sue Miner, Mark Brownell and Mary Lou Chlipala

Acknowledgements

A very early version of *Orchidelirium* was workshopped in 1999 at the Barrington Stage Company, in Great Barrington, Massachusetts. Andrew Volkoff directed.

Pea Green Productions has been the prime developer of *Orchidelirium* since then. An initial reading with Mark Brownell, Sue Miner, Sean Baek, Lois Lorimer and Maureen Kirkpatrick was held in early fall, 2001. In October, 2001, a full workshop was held, with actors Martha Burns, Anthony Malarky, Stephen Ouimette and Anne Page. Sue Miner directed, Mark Brownell was dramaturg and Sandy Plunkett was Stage Manager. The workshop culminated in a public reading on Saturday, October 27, 2001.

In May, 2002, *Orchidelirium* was included in the Festival of New Works at the University of Michigan in Ann Arbor. The cast consisted of Joseph Hendrix (Mike); Pamela Lewis (Frances); Lorijean Nichols (Alice); and Malcolm Tulip (Arthur). Sue Miner directed. Callie McKee stage managed. Other contributors included Mark Allen Berg (Lighting Designer); Rich Lindsey (Props and Set); Clark Johnson (Sound Design); Katie Conrad (ASM); Rebecca Valentino (Costumes) and Anup Aurora (ME/Assistant Lighting Design.) The Artistic Producer of the Festival is John Neville-Andrews and the Managing Director is Mary Lou Chlipala, who also gave dramaturgical advice during the development of the script.

Special thanks to Mark Brownell, whose dramaturgical contribution has been considerable and greatly appreciated, and to Katherine Burkman and Steve Wargo for their support and feedback.

What's True and What Isn't

Orchidelirium is a mix of fictionalized fact, and factualized fiction... There was indeed a Joseph Paxton who revolutionized the care and treatment of orchids, but he died long before anyone in this play could have known him. There was also an American Acclimatization Society, but the locus of its ornithological crime was not Pittsburgh, but New York City's Central Park. Vast liberties have been taken with the Frick name. The family was real enough, but my particular fractious Frick never existed, nor did any of the other ladies who regularly succumbed to orchidelirium at the O'Keefe Conservatory. Technology has been corrupted to serve this play; not even the inventive Alice could have sent trans-Atlantic telegrams in 1895. Finally, there is no pharmaceutical company named Vitakampf, but there are plenty of real corporations steering the course of academic inquiry at our universities. For these and other small liberties, I plead dramatic licence.

Characters

1895

ALICE O'Keefe:	33. A highly inventive, amateur orchidologist.
ARTHUR Fox:	A bit older. English, with a travelling accent.

Today

Dr. FRANCES O'Keefe:	40ish. Great-great niece of Alice. A professor of Ethnobotany.
MIKE:	25. Baptist missionary and orchid hunter.

Setting

Primarily

The Orchid House at the O'Keefe Conservatory, Pittsburgh, Pennsylvania. Originally built for Alice O'Keefe by her father in 1890, the conservatory is now owned and administered by the University. The O'Keefe is open to the public; proceeds from admission fees and special events help with its upkeep. The monies raised also help to fund the small portion of the conservatory that is used by Frances as a research lab, on sufferance of the university.

Other

The Orchid House, Kew Gardens, London England.

The upper reaches of the Orinoco River, near the Venezuela-Brazil border

The university office of Dean Fulton

Time

1895 and now.

Production Information

Orchidelirium premiered on February 21, 2003 at the Factory Theatre Studio in Toronto, in a Pea Green/Theatre Voce Co-production, with the following cast and crew:

ARTHUR: Patrick Galligan
MIKE: Joel Hechter
FRANCES: Tanja Jacobs
ALICE: Anne Page

Director: Sue Miner
Producer: Mark Brownell
Set Design: Brenda Guldenstein
Lighting Design: Michael Kruse
Costume Design: Nina Okens
Sound Design: Darren Copeland
Design Assistant: Junko Yamaguchi
Stage Manager: Trina A. Sookhai
Production Manager: Rick Banville

Funding assistance for the writing of *Orchidelirium* has been received from the Laidlaw Foundation. The Toronto Arts Council, Ontario Arts Council and The Canada Council for the Arts have all assisted with production funding.

The Theatre Voce-Pea Green production of *Orchidelirium* was nominated for three Dora Mavor Moore awards, including Best New Play.

Dave Carley

Dave Carley's plays have been produced across Canada, the United States and around the world. He writes primarily for stage, but has also been produced on radio and television, and his journalism has been published in a variety of newspapers and magazines. Dave Carley's website is www.davecarley.com.

Act One

Black.

Light comes up on the orchid room of the O'Keefe Conservatory, as secular Christmas muzak plays.

Amid the orchids, a Victorian cardboard tableau becomes visible—a small group of carollers dressed for a winter's wassail. The tableau is a bit worn and tatty, in the manner of a much-loved Christmas ornament.

As the light grows on the conservatory, it becomes apparent that the tableau is at cross-seasonal purposes with the wild profusion of orchids. Lights begin to twinkle through the orchids. It's all rather pretty, in a somewhat excessive fashion.

One of the carollers—FRANCES—reaches out and pulls a plug. The Christmas lights and music cut out immediately. FRANCES turns to the audience.

FRANCES: Merry fucking Christmas. Let me elaborate. Merry fucking Victorian Christmas. And welcome. Welcome to the O'Keefe Conservatory.

FRANCES moves out of the tableau. As she speaks, she puts up more wreaths, bells, bows, boughs and periodically blasts everything—including herself—with spray-on snow.

So—did you have a pleasant ride here? D'you detour around that construction on Forbes—or did your Beamers and Benzes and Lexi plow on through? And just to visit little old moi! In my annual cameo as nutty professor gussied up like—who—Mary Todd Lincoln in a—what—a Martha Stewart wet-dream. My annual twelve days of infamy. Aw, come to me, you coddled masses. Bring me your aching wallets. 'Tis the jolly old season after all.

FRANCES moves back to the tableau, spraying snow on ALICE as she passes her. ALICE moves out of the tableau, holding an orchid. ALICE addresses her friends.

ALICE: Cattleya labiata. Miss Frick says donating these to the widows of Civil War veterans is moronic. They don't have enough coal to heat their houses—why would they want orchids? Miss Duryea's idea of knitting mufflers for the widows is also out of the question. None of us can knit. Miss Mellon wanted to set up a soup kitchen for the poor but this too has been vetoed—again by Miss Frick. "Soup is the lubricant of labour unrest." What then are we to do?

ALICE freezes back into the tableau. FRANCES moves forward again.

FRANCES: The O'Keefe Conservatory was built in 1890 by my great-great grandfather, Wallace O'Keefe. *(Indicates an older cardboard man in the tableau.)* The stove magnate. That's not the same as a fridge magnate.

FRANCES waits for a laugh, which she either doesn't get or is of insufficient volume.

Excuse me folks—that was my one big joke? O'Keefe Self-Timing Electric Stoves! Wallace O'Keefe made five goddamn million of them in his factory on the Allegheny, and he shipped them all over the continent, to wherever there was a woman sweating over a wood stove.

ALICE: *(From tableau.)* What are we to do?

FRANCES: Picture that: thoroughly modern husband shows up one day with an enamel miracle that doesn't chew wood and actually has a real clock built right into it.

ALICE: We have so much time

FRANCES: —A stove that cuts hours off his wife's work week

ALICE: —We have so much money

FRANCES: —My great-great grandfather gave American women the luxury of time. An extra hour a day. And then he turned around and gave his poor daughter Alice—who already had all the time in the world—he gave her this.

ALICE: *(Moving out of tableau again.)* There must be something we can do with all this beauty. Something that won't promote unionism or socialism or Fabianism—Miss Frick, have I left out any isms?

FRANCES: If you're going to snicker about Aunt Alice, go do it elsewhere. Not here, not amidst her orchids.

ALICE: Ask England. That's the answer. I'll write Sir Joseph Paxton. I'll ask: Your Sir-ship, what can an idle of American spinsters do to better the world? *(Begins writing.)* He might have an idea. The English occasionally do get ideas.

FRANCES: *(Stops at a particularly vivid orchid and her guard immediately drops.)* It's a rolfea. Rolfea. Sounds like a kind of therapy, doesn't it. This was named after Robert Rolfe, co-author of—get this—'The Orchid Stud Book'. This was the first registered hybrid in America. 1907. Alice was already a laughingstock by then—she'd screwed up the nation's ecosystem, and she was too embarrassed to go out in public.

ALICE: March 23, 1895. Dear Sir. Dear Sir Sir. I hope you remember me. I'm writing to you again, not as a kindred lover of orchids this time, but as the agent of a group of top-notch American ladies. Our little club includes Miss Mellon (banking), Miss Duryea (carriages), and the Misses Willett (fine furniture and coffins). And Miss Frick. She's the one who marched through Europe in a ferocious quest for a title. *(Erasing latter.)* Oh, that's uncharitable.

FRANCES: —Alice hid in here. Collecting, cataloguing—corresponding with her fellow orchid lovers... And you know what? Last month a group of Germans visited this place, just to see this orchid! So maybe Aunt Alice wasn't so wacky after all. When was the last time a bunch of Germans came to see something in your house?

Light has been slowly coming up on ARTHUR, whom the audience will initially assume is Paxton. He is working with orchids. He pulls a letter from his pocket and reads it.

ALICE: We are infected—oh, infected?—suffused with the spirit of charity. But we can neither knit nor ladle. My orchids are of no use to the poor. We're stumped. I've heard you're doing pioneering work with exotic animals, under the auspices of the English Acclimatization—Lord, how's that spelled—English Acclimatization Society.

ARTHUR: *(Coming over.)* "English Acclimatization Society".

ALICE: You're cooking and eating foreign animals—all for the future benefit of your countrymen. Is there something similar we might do here in America? Yours with kind regards, Alice O'Keefe."

Light off ARTHUR.

At the very least he might send me another orchid.

ALICE ventures off into her orchids.

FRANCES: *(Of another orchid.)* Cymbidium Devonianum. I might hybridize it. Just for fun. I can create something that even God didn't imagine. And then I'll clone it. Make thousands of copies. *(Points out gift shop.)* For sale in the gift shop.

FRANCES's cellphone has begun ringing.

Excuse me folks. Where the hell... *(She retrieves it from her costume with some difficulty.)* Kind of destroys the Victorian illusion, doesn't it. *(Answers.)* O'Keefe. Hello? Hello?

Light up on MIKE. He's hanging upside down in the Venezuelan jungle. FRANCES moves away from her visitors to take the call.

MIKE: Hello?

FRANCES: Hello?

MIKE: Doctor O'Keefe?

FRANCES: Yes—Mike? Is that you?

MIKE: Hey doc—how's life?

FRANCES: How's life?

MIKE: Yeah, how's life.

FRANCES: Well, I've hung the wreaths. I'm burning cinnamon; the parking lot's got bows hanging from the lights like—bloodclots. I've sprayed sparkle on my tits and any minute now I've got a busload of Shriners coming in from Akron. You sound strange.

MIKE: I'm upside-down.

FRANCES: Why?

MIKE: 'Cause I'm here.

FRANCES: Where's "here"? Mike—are you—do you have something to tell me?

MIKE: Yup.

FRANCES: You're serious?

MIKE: Yup.

FRANCES: You're actually going to whisper those three special words?

MIKE: Uh huh—

FRANCES: I've paid a lot for those three words—

MIKE: Excuse me? You haven't paid us a thing yet! But hang on, stay on the line.

MIKE pulls a knife from his belt and light goes off him. ALICE bursts by FRANCES, waving a letter. Light will soon come up on ARTHUR, formally dressed.

ALICE: Ladies! Ladies! Listen. Shh. *(Reads.)* "May the First, 1895. Dear Miss O'Keefe. I'm about to embark on an orchid-gathering expedition to the Orinoco."

ARTHUR: *(With last.)* To the Orinoco.

ALICE: Orinoco. That's a river in South America. I looked it up. "In my absence I have asked my colleague"

ARTHUR: —My trusted colleague

ALICE: —"Arthur Fox"

ARTHUR: —Timlin

ALICE: —"Arthur Fox-Timlin to maintain my correspondence and advise you on all things orchidological and philanthropical."

ARTHUR: Just as he so advises me. Sincerely, Paxton.

ARTHUR flips a serving towel over his forearm, as the light goes off him and ALICE. Light is back up on MIKE. He's right-side up now, but clinging to the cliff.

MIKE: Stand by.

FRANCES: That's two words. You promised three.

MIKE: *(Reaching unsuccessfully with his knife.)* Heck—I'm going to have to climb some more. I'll call you right back.

MIKE puts cell away. Light off him.

FRANCES: Dear God, let this be it. *(Looks outside.)* Damn, the Shriners!

FRANCES hurries off to greet the bus tour. Focus back on ALICE and ARTHUR. ALICE is working on another letter. The letter convention begins to segue into dialogue.

ALICE: Dear Mr. Fox-Timlin. I'm relieved that Sir Joseph didn't just dash off to the Orinoco and leave his orchids unattended. He was so generous to me—once. He sent me that lovely cattleya...

ARTHUR: I will send you more.

ALICE: Oh I wasn't hinting

ARTHUR: —And I'll enclose instructions for their care, which I have uh developed with the collaboration of Sir Joseph.

ARTHUR is diverted by a tinkling bell.

ALICE: I did have that other question, too. What might a small group of excessively rich and idle spinsters do to benefit mankind?

ARTHUR: *(Trying to leave.)* That is a new dilemma for me. We have our Acclimatization Society, of course. But eating wild beasts might not be suitable for the fairer sex. I will give this serious thought. Yours truly. Arthur Fox. Dash. Timlin. Esquire.

ARTHUR heads off in the bell's direction.

Postscript. Please send future correspondence to me at the London post box below, rather than Kew. It's more efficient.

ARTHUR exits. Light off ALICE. FRANCES has returned.

FRANCES: Dear, dear Akron Shriners. Dearest of all service groups. I'm so sad you all came in a bus—I was expecting you to show up in those sexy little go karts. Now. I have to make an important call of a botanic nature, so why don't you check out the gift shop. Yes—that way…

FRANCES moves off, dialing her cell phone. Light up on MIKE. He's in an awkward position and moving towards something. The cell rings and he answers it with difficulty.

MIKE: What!?

FRANCES: You said you'd phone right back.

MIKE: I'm halfway up a cliff.

FRANCES: I only want three words—three words so I can have this goddamn place to myself again. Three words so I can wipe off the fucking sparkle paint and

MIKE: —You have a really foul mouth.

FRANCES: Your point?

MIKE: —For a professor.

FRANCES: Professors can't swear?

MIKE: It's unscientific.

FRANCES: You're a bit of a prig.

MIKE: I just don't think it's cool to swear all the time. I also think you're doing it just to bug me.

FRANCES: Right, right you're a man of God.

MIKE: I'm also the one in the middle of the jungle finding you a flower. But... *(Reaching with one arm.)* Stand by for the three special words.

FRANCES: Pardon

MIKE: —Because I think, I really think… *(Pulls a branch towards himself.)* Doctor O'Keefe?

FRANCES: Yes?

MIKE: I—found—it.

FRANCES: You found it?

MIKE: Yes ma'am.

FRANCES: *(Sinking to her knees in gratitude.)* Oh, he's found it he's found it—

Meanwhile MIKE has pulled the branch closer to him and is sniffing. Something is wrong. FRANCES stops celebrating.

Mike? You there? Why aren't you talking? Mike?

MIKE: I don't know.

FRANCES: What don't you know.

MIKE: Maybe it's not it.

FRANCES: But you just said—

MIKE: —It's darn close. It's the right colour and right

location according to Paxton's journal. Cliff face, lithophytic, it's blue but *(Sniffs.)* there's no scent.

FRANCES: The smell is supposed to be its most obvious characteristic.

MIKE: I know I know

FRANCES: —Paxton was very clear about that in his journal. He said it reeked like a dead fucking cow.

MIKE: I was premature. My guides were pointing at it and I assumed—it's very lovely. But sorry. No three words yet.

Light off MIKE. FRANCES cries out in despair and throws her cellphone across the conservatory. It nearly nails ALICE. A window smashes, off. A bird thuds into the conservatory at the same time. FRANCES exits, to search for her phone. ALICE picks up the bird—an Eastern Bluebird—from the conservatory floor.

ALICE: Hello, Sialia Sialis. Eastern Bluebird. Male, mature. Rusty breast like an old stove. And your back—this blue—what is it? Cerulean? How to describe it. Dear Mr. Fox-Timlin. What is the colour of the sky over Capri? I'll never see it, so you tell me. Is it anything like the blue of my foundling? Feather enclosed.

Light up on ARTHUR, examining feather.

ARTHUR: My dear Miss O'Keefe, a sky is a sky is just a sky.

ALICE: Dear Mr. Fox-Timlin, sometimes a sky can fail to be a sky at all. Take the one we have here, in Pittsburgh. The mills make short work of blue. The air is so thick that my father and brothers take extra shirts to work, so they can change into clean ones at midday. We have to wash the conservatory constantly. I have a boy who does nothing else. He starts at one end and by the time he's at the other, he has to begin all over again.

ARTHUR: *(Impressed.)* How large is your conservatory?

ALICE: Sir Joseph hasn't told you? It's over 100,000 square feet and we have plans to expand. We're the biggest west of Philadelphia.

ARTHUR: And it was a gift from your father?

ALICE: I'm 29. 31. 31 hovering perilously close to 34. This place is my father's substitute for the dowry I'm saving him. Chur-wi. Chur-wi. Tru-ly. Tru-ly. I'm imitating a bluebird. I hope that's not too eccentric. Ar-thur? May I call you Arthur, Mr. Fox-Timlin?

ARTHUR: Yes—Ma'am.

ALICE: Alice.

ARTHUR: Alice.

Light off ARTHUR. FRANCES is addressing a new bus tour.

FRANCES: —And you're from—where—Dayton? My, this is quite the week for Ohio. Yesterday, I had two busloads of Akronistas. Welcome to my yuletide hell. My Aunt Alice's conservatory. She couldn't travel, you know. No little bus jaunts for her. She couldn't visit any of the other conservatories that were being established all over the continent.

ALICE returns. She may have a nurse's cap. The bird is in a box.

She had to rely on people coming here—orchid lovers.

ARTHUR: Alice, I meant to ask you in my last letter, why can't you come to England?

ALICE: I can't tolerate motion. It's my little cross.

ARTHUR: So you really won't—can't visit.

ALICE: No.

ARTHUR: Ever.

ALICE: I'm stuck.

ARTHUR seems relieved.

FRANCES: I found her letters and, in them, she talked of the causes of her isolation, describing it as a physical ailment, but today we know it to be something far more complex.

ALICE: Last summer I tried to take the train to Latrobe—it's cool there

FRANCES: —Once, desperate to escape the air

ARTHUR: *(Reading a letter.)* —"But I nearly died after two miles."

ALICE: We were barely out of the city and they had to pull over on a siding

FRANCES: —Apparently, she was carried off the train.

ALICE: They dismantled one of the sleeping compartments and made me a bed, right there. I lay in the field and prepared to die.

FRANCES: She lay in state amidst the cows—just Alice

ALICE: —Just me and my maid. Eventually the sky stopped wheeling and a farmer appeared with a wagon. We waved the train on, I lay in the wagon

ARTHUR: *(Reading.)*—"And we bumped back to Pittsburgh." *(His letter.)* They stopped an entire train just because you felt sick?

ALICE: My father owns the railroad.

FRANCES: Carriages and boats also made her puke.

ALICE: *(With FRANCES.)*—Puke. Do you use that word, Arthur? Shakespeare did, so I suppose you must, constantly. It's not a pretty word but it exactly describes what happens to me the second I try travelling anywhere I can't walk. *(Moving off.)* Come on Mr. Bluebird, we must find you water.

ALICE moves off. ARTHUR resumes working. FRANCES continues to address the bus tour.

FRANCES: She never saw Latrobe or Capri… Those places had to come to her, to here. Luckily, Alice was rich enough to import the orchids of the world; she worked by trial and error, she also used Paxton's journal—but a lot of it was sheer instinct. Alice became famous—infamous?—for her insane orchids. *(Holds up a flamboyant flower.)* If there's ever been a case study for orchidelirium: Epidendra Okeefiana. Named in her honour by the American Orchid Society. Available in the gift shop.

ALICE returns with water. She will baptize the bird. ARTHUR is reading this account.

ALICE: I'm christening him Stanley. In England's honour. After Sir Henry Morton Stanley. That witty man. Imagine slopping through a million miles of African jungle—going where no Stanley had ever before gone—and when he finally encounters another European, he has the good humour to say, "Dr. Livingstone, I presume."

ARTHUR: *(With her above line.)* "Dr. Livingstone, I presume."

FRANCES's cellphone rings. Focus off ALICE and ARTHUR. Light up on MIKE, who is sitting with a McDonald's bag, having lunch. FRANCES answers. At this point, the phone convention can start to disappear in the same way the letter-writing one did.

FRANCES: Why are you calling?

MIKE: May the Lord shower his bounty upon you, Doc.

FRANCES: Where are you.

MIKE: I'm back in town. San Fernando. The town where my mission is? My real job? Fric and Frac were getting antsy.

FRANCES: Fric and Frac?

MIKE: My guides?

FRANCES: Right right—

MIKE: They want to see their families.

FRANCES: How sweet.

MIKE: And get paid. And oh, I wanted to check my e-mails. Administer communion. And get paid.

FRANCES: You haven't found the orchid.

MIKE: That's not the deal—this isn't C.O.D. Listen, I'm walking a fine line here. I'm not supposed to be making field trips into the rain forest with the local lowlifes. I'm supposed to be

FRANCES: —I know what you're supposed to be doing. What do you want to do—that's the question.

MIKE: I want to find that orchid.

FRANCES: That's my boy.

MIKE: There's another swamp slightly south of the one I was just in. That might be it. We're heading out first thing tomorrow but it would sure help if I had the money—I have to pay the guys—

FRANCES pushes her phone's off button. Black on MIKE.

FRANCES: —Oops. Disconnected. *(Moves to window.)* That'll work just once. *(Looks out.)* Shit, another tour bus.

ALICE has also moved to the window. She opens it and holds STANLEY up to it.

ALICE: A bird in the house is bad luck but you're a bluebird in a green-house so maybe that doesn't apply. Still, you have to leave. Shoo. Off with you Stanley. Chur-wi. Fly. Why won't you go? Is it your wing? Or is it my flowers? *(Moves off through flowers, showing them to Stanley.)*

FRANCES: *(To visitors again.)* There's a medical term for what we feel—those of you whose hearts are beating a little hard right now. It's called 'orchidelirium'. Your heart beats too fast, you feel a little flushed, maybe your mouth is dry… yeah? You know what I'm talking about?

Orchidelirium. I've lost two husbands to it. With Husband Number One—Jimmy—it was his orchidelirium, not mine. In retrospect I think there were other deliriums at play too, because while I was off teaching, Jimmy was tiptoeing through the orchids. And not alone.

Husband Number Two was also a Jimmy. But where Jimmy One was floral, Jimmy Two was bland. And how you can reconcile bland with this? I began to resent going home at night—is this too much information? I thought not. This is partly why you come, isn't it. OK, so we're lying in bed, me and Jimmy Two and I'm listening to his regular breathing and by regular, well, you could set an atomic clock by it. I'm lying there and I begin imagining him with other parts—this professor's chin, that professor's eyes, that student's butt. And next, different colours: a stripe of blue down his back. Orange chevrons up his thighs. One oversized purple anther. Oh God—I was hybridizing him!

Jimmy got the house and contents, and I came back here—alone, broke, and orchidelirious. And that's how I've stayed. OK. Enough of the tabloid stuff—thanks for coming, folks. *(Points.)* Check out the gift shop, this way…

FRANCES exits. Focus on ALICE watching Stanley.

ALICE: Chur-wi. There are no predators in here, my dear, just one anthropomorphic spinster. Chur-wi. I won't be eating Stanley pie… Though, speaking of predators—

ARTHUR has entered.

What is your Acclimatization Society dining on this week?

ARTHUR: Cassowary. We're celebrating Sir Joseph's return from the Orinoco.

ALICE: How lucky you are! Cassowary and Sir Joseph Paxton, at the same table. We call Paxton 'The Prince of Gardeners'! I am irrigated exactly to his specifications.

ARTHUR: How is Stanley?

ALICE: It's very strange, Arthur. He doesn't bother trying to fly anymore. He just—hops.

ARTHUR: It's wrong for a songbird to live like that. He needs a challenge. The original Stanley crossed the Congo. At the very least, your Stanley should brave Pittsburgh. Hippity-hop home. His wife and children—think of their poor broken birdhearts.

ALICE: "Broken birdhearts"—I'm not quite that dotty. Am I, Stan-ley. *(To ARTHUR.)* Please don't patronize me, Arthur.

A ringing phone sends them into black. Light up on FRANCES and MIKE.

FRANCES: Where are you now?

MIKE: Back on the river.

FRANCES: Did Fric and Frac—

MIKE: I had a heck of a time persuading them to come, without pay.

FRANCES: I wired money yesterday.

MIKE: To where.

FRANCES: *(Beat.)* San Hernando.

MIKE: Hernando.

FRANCES: Yes.

MIKE: Because I'm in San Fernando.

FRANCES: Spanish is so confusing.

MIKE: You've memorized the Latin names for every orchid and you can't… Listen Doc, there has to be money when I get back or you aren't getting whatever it is I'm finding. Understand?

FRANCES: Is that a threat?

MIKE: I'm a missionary.

FRANCES: That's a non-sequitur.

MIKE: Missionaries don't make threats. We state facts.

FRANCES: Missionaries have changed!

MIKE: Well, I guess facts can be threatening. Like: no money, no orchid. And you can take that fact to the bank.

Light off MIKE. FRANCES moves off, and begins taking down Victorian Christmas decorations and replacing them with New Year's ones. Light comes back up on ARTHUR.

ARTHUR: I didn't mean to sound patronizing. I'm so sorry Alice

ALICE moves on.

ALICE: —Apology accepted. By the way, I've just grafted a cattleya to the red oak at the park gates. It has completely confused the squirrels.

ARTHUR: I'm so happy you're not angry. And congratulations on the graft.

ALICE: Oh, I laughed at your last line. "Congratulations on the graft." That means something very different in this city. Arthur, one of my sisters in the American Acclimatization Society—for that is what we're now calling ourselves—has a question for you. Miss Frick demands to know if you've ever eaten cat.

FRANCES has exited.

ARTHUR: Cat?

ALICE: In the course of your Society's research.

ARTHUR: We eat many kinds of animals in our effort to broaden the English diet. In the cat family: jaguar, tiger and lynx.

ALICE: Nothing domestic?

ARTHUR: Oh, nothing domestic. Though I've been tempted by some Soho Persians. Tonight, by the way, we're eating python. When skinned and roasted, I'm told it's like chicken. Next week, it's zebra. But Alice—if you've appropriated our title—what does that mean? You'll be dining on skunk?

ALICE: The American Acclimatization Society is not going to actually eat things. Our focus will be more vegetarian. Less violent. *(Looks out.)* No! No! Go away!

ALICE runs out. There is a boom. FRANCES falls backwards into the conservatory. The rifle falls with her. ALICE and ARTHUR disappear with the boom.

FRANCES: Fucking starlings! By God I'll kill you all!

Her cellphone begins ringing. Light up on MIKE.

MIKE: Happy New Year.

FRANCES: Like hell it is!

MIKE: Let's start again. Happy New Year.

FRANCES: And let's clarify. It's not. There's a thousand starlings covering this place in shit. The Gay Nineties New Year's Gala was a fiasco.

MIKE: You said tickets were sold out!

FRANCES: Yeah, and all morning I've been finding cigarettes butted in my orchids and someone stole a fern and—why are you phoning?

MIKE: I'm in a swamp.

FRANCES: That's real nice.

MIKE: Make that: Paxton's Swamp.

FRANCES: How do you know it's Paxton's swamp? You said that about the last three.

MIKE: Everything matches up this time. There's a cliff on the far side. Just like he wrote. There's a small open lake fronting it. Remember—he described it as a castle and a moat

FRANCES: —OK OK, keep the phone dry. Call me the second you get to the cliff. Wait—Mike—can you see anything growing on it?

MIKE: No flowers, not from here—but there's definitely vegetation.

FRANCES: The orchids are lithophytic. They'll be growing right off the rock face

MIKE: —I know I know

FRANCES: —Mike. Be careful.

MIKE: I'm always careful.

FRANCES: I'm serious. And watch Fric and Frac. They may get antsy about harvesting the orchids.

MIKE: They haven't so far.

FRANCES: Yeah, well, watch 'em.

MIKE: Why?

FRANCES: In Paxton's day, the natives thought the plants were sacred. Bye.

MIKE: Wait. You never told me that.

FRANCES: I didn't?

MIKE: No, you didn't.

FRANCES: I uh must have forgotten.

MIKE: Like you forgot the cheque?

FRANCES: I have a lot on my mind! Bye.

FRANCES hangs up. MIKE immediately dials her back.

MIKE: When you said "sacred" what exactly did you mean?

FRANCES: Sacred. No big deal. OK, they were going to kill Paxton if he picked any. But that was a century ago. If Fric and Frac have lost the knowledge, well, obviously, don't give it back to them.

FRANCES hangs up. MIKE immediately dials her back.

MIKE: Doctor, why are the orchids sacred? The colour? The smell?

FRANCES: Yeah. Yes. Both. Good luck—

FRANCES shuts off cell. Light off MIKE also. ALICE returns with a dead bluebird. ARTHUR finds the journal. As ALICE speaks, ARTHUR steals the journal.

ALICE: Stanley is dead. The park is full of feral cats. I put Stanley on a low branch and they climbed up and got him. Stanley saw them coming but he thought they were just some new breed of spinster. When Stanley was alive I had a mission. A tiny mission, yes, but now? Arthur, please don't take this the wrong way. We're Americans. We like being rich, but once we get there we also have this odd habit of asking, "Now what?" The ladies are getting restless.

FRANCES returns to the conservatory and sits beside ALICE. She pulls out a book identical to the one ARTHUR is holding, and then she turns to address ALICE, for the first time. ALICE doesn't register her presence, however.

FRANCES: I always knew it was in here. The answer. In this remarkable journal he gave you. Paxton's meticulous record of flowers grown, hybrids completed, bizarre beasts eaten... his journeys to the tropics... This was my best and most private adventure story, my own personal Nancy Drew, the one legacy of Alice that we've managed to keep in our family... And, in it, Paxton's account of finding the orchid of all orchids.

Except, a hundred years later, there's hardly a soul left who thinks there's anything of medicinal value in the rain forest. Medicine: it's just chemistry now.

MIKE is reading to Fric and Frac from a small Bible.

MIKE: There's a line in 'Proverbs' about pride. We should be concerned about that, guys, because we could become famous. If this orchid is as special as she says it is, then we're going to be as famous as Sir Edmund Hilary and that guy he climbed Mount Everest with. *(Strains for name.)* The Sherpa. *(Looking.)* OK, where is it—

FRANCES: Look Alice—see that building? When it's finished, it'll put us completely in shade. It's being paid for by Vitakampf—the pharmaceutical company. Swedish. With tentacles all over the world. Vitakampf—our university's new best friend, the one who calls the research shots. And what will they do over there? Oh, split cells, play around with embryos, poke at fetuses... We supply the chemists, they get the copyrights—and to hell with the rest of us.

MIKE: 'Proverbs 16'. "Pride goeth before destruction and a haughty spirit before a fall." That doesn't mean I'm going to fall off the cliff. This'll be a piece of cake. There's a climbing rock three times this high at Disneyworld.

FRANCES: I know that orchid's there. I can't travel to it because I've got your genes, Alice. But I found someone, on the internet of all places, a young innocent who also believes...

MIKE: God put those orchids there for a reason. He made them hard to find—that was for another reason. So they'd still be here, waiting for us. To harvest. Ready guys?

Focus off MIKE. FRANCES exits. ALICE turns to ARTHUR.

ALICE: I've had Stanley stuffed. Birds die so easily. They're more fragile than orchids. How was the zebra?

ARTHUR: *(Consults the journal.)* The zebra. *(Finds reference.)* "Gristly. But properly marinaded—a bit like chicken." Alice, your last letters have sounded—very disconsolate.

ALICE: Oh, Arthur, why can't I just be? Why can't I just stay here and work with my orchids and—why isn't it enough! Why do I feel—why am I

ARTHUR: —Perhaps it's just the winter doldrums. With spring around the bend

ALICE: —But I've had 29 winters already, and I've never felt this way.

ARTHUR: When I'm frustrated—when an orchid refuses to flower or a zebra is gristly, I turn to poetry.

ALICE: You do?

ARTHUR: Of course. Why are you surprised?

ALICE: I'm not really—it's just—it's what I do, too. Whose poetry?

ARTHUR: "It was a lover and his lass,
With a hey, and a ho, and a hey nonino..."

ALICE: Shakespeare! "That o'er the green corn-field did pass."

ARTHUR: "In the spring time, the only pretty ring time,
When the birds do sing time."

ALICE & ARTHUR: "Hey ding a ding time
Sweet lovers love the spring..."

ALICE: You grew up with that. With Shakespeare. We didn't, alas. I can't turn a corner and be walking where he walked—or see a tree he saw, hear a bird he heard...

ARTHUR: "Tu whit; the answer will come..."

ALICE: I wonder if it will. *(Moving off.)* I wonder—

ARTHUR returns to the journal. FRANCES reappears holding Paxton's journal as well. ALICE moves through the conservatory, gently, sotto, identifying her orchids.

FRANCES: *(Reading and descending into orchidelirium.)* "It took us twelve weeks to make our way up the Orinoco, by steamer. It broke down repeatedly—if the boiler wasn't dying, then we were foundering on a rock or log."

ARTHUR: *(Also reading.)* "The river was impassible above San Fernando, so we transferred to canoe, and we paddled further upstream, me the sole European, escorted by six surly natives."

MIKE: They're nervous. The jungle fills them with dread. If I hadn't promised them major bucks I know they'd take off.

FRANCES: "And then, when we reached the headwaters, four of them deserted. It didn't seem to be another tribe they feared—in fact, the entire region seemed bereft of humans. The remaining two guides—they were younger, less superstitious, or so I thought. "

ARTHUR: "We built a raft and began the final leg, through seemingly endless swamps, interminable tracts of bog and water… but never did my guides falter. They knew where to go."

MIKE: This swamp is louder and hotter. Oh man, snakes!

FRANCES: "They hang from the trees, their skin glistening, oily, glinting as they coil and uncoil, straighten and flex, thick ropes of corded muscle."

MIKE: I—don't—like—snakes!

ARTHUR: "And birds like no man has seen before, cries that have never been heard…"

FRANCES: "The last swamp is a mile wide and it swarms with dolphins."

Faintly, a bell begins ringing in the background. Only ARTHUR will—eventually—register its sound.

MIKE: Dolphins!

FRANCES: "Ice white dolphins."

ARTHUR: "No bigger than a woman's thigh."

FRANCES: "Alabaster."

MIKE: They're swimming at us!

ARTHUR: "And then they dart away, as if *(Distracted now by bell.)*

FRANCES: "As if repulsed by a magnetic field."

MIKE: They're blind! They've got no eyes! Look! There's a fold of skin where their eyes should be—OK steady guys, we're nearly there!

FRANCES: "My guides pole on. They are terrified now but I am beside myself with excitement."

MIKE: The cliff is awesome!

ARTHUR: "Like Table Mountain."

MIKE: I can climb that—no sweat!

FRANCES: "And as it draws closer I see orchids, cascading all over its face."

ARTHUR: "It's as if I'd awoken from a fevered dream and found myself on the tip of Africa…"

ALICE is overcome and has stopped reciting orchid names.

FRANCES: "My guides point and begin chattering wildly in

their primitive tongue. The cliff face itself rises only fifty feet."

Light full on MIKE, who has climbed up to the orchids. He snips one off. He pulls it to himself, sniffs and recoils violently.

MIKE: Gee. Gee. OK. Wow. *(Sniffs again.)* Wow.

MIKE pulls out his phone. The bell is now ringing loudly offstage and ARTHUR runs in its direction. FRANCES's cell is ringing. She desperately pats her pockets and finds it.

FRANCES: Mike?

MIKE: I-found-it.

Bell ringing clear, off.

ARTHUR: *(Exiting.)* At once, yes! Coming!

ALICE: *(Coming out of swoon.)* Eureka!

FRANCES: You found it?

MIKE: I found it!

ALICE: Eureka!

FRANCES: You really found it?

MIKE: This time, yes. For sure. Yes.

Light off MIKE. FRANCES falls to her knees.

FRANCES: Thank God.

FRANCES begins to weep. Light up on ALICE, who is pacing excitedly around the conservatory. Light up on ARTHUR.

ALICE: Dear Arthur, I have it! The answer. And it is so simple—it came to me as I was—napping. I will combine the best of what you do with the best of what I do.

ARTHUR: *(To himself.)* She's going to eat orchids?

ALICE: I'll import birds. Not to eat. But yes, for a diet, the workers' diet. For their spiritual diet!

ARTHUR: *(To himself.)* Surely they have enough birds in America already!

ALICE: I told you I can't ride, but I do walk, everywhere, and yesterday I hiked down to the river, all the way thinking about you walking in Shakespeare's exact footsteps and me not having that privilege and then there I was, near the mills and, over at the bank I could hear voices. Rough voices. I should have turned away—my father has expressly forbidden me to go near the mills—but Arthur, what did I see? Six workers, feeding their lunches to a family of ducks!

ARTHUR: *(To himself.)* Is she barmy?

ALICE: And now it strikes me! Why not have birds here, birds here, among my orchids! Why not go a step further than that, even? Why not connect those birds with something greater? Greater than orchids—if that's possible. If ordinary ducks can exert such appeal that millworkers will share their lunches with them—why not present them with birds that will in turn feed their minds?

ARTHUR: *(To himself.)* She has gone mad!

ALICE: —Why not surround them with: the birds of the Bard! Shakepeare's birds! Here! In my conservatory! Birds—which they love. And Shakespeare—whom they should love. Here! Oh Arthur, this is a project upon which we, the ladies of the American Acclimatization Society, are in full agreement.

ARTHUR: *(To himself.)* Shakespeare's birds?

ALICE: Or at least we will be, when I tell them this

afternoon. Because we stand united in our admiration of Shakespeare. Especially those who haven't read his works.

ARTHUR: *(To himself, getting germ of an idea.)* But Shakespeare's birds are here.

ALICE: *(With him.)*—But Shakespeare's birds are there. As was Shakespeare. But we read him here, we adore him here. If Shakespeare had managed to live an extra century or two he might well have visited America. Mr. Dickens did. And oh—Mr. Wilde gave a brilliant lecture last year. It influenced us dreadfully. We talked in epigrams for over a week. It was a struggle for Miss Frick, who favours the blunt. I'm getting away from my point. Arthur, dearest Arthur—who gives an owl's hoot that the corporeal Shakespeare never graced these shores! His plays have—and so can his birds!

ARTHUR: But how can his birds get there, from here?

ALICE: You have so much experience importing anteaters, cassowaries, python… surely exporting a bird or two would be a lead pipe cinch! Will you be my agent?

ARTHUR: I—uh—could arrange for birds to be caught, netted. And I could ship them, they'd need special cages and

ALICE: —How much?

ARTHUR: I beg your pardon?

ALICE: How can I put this delicately? I'm American, I can't. How much money do you want?

ARTHUR: Oh I couldn't accept—it would be a favour.

ALICE: Nonsense. I won't have you spending your own money. Tell me how much.

ARTHUR: *(Too fast.)* I need a gameskeeper and there are the cages and nets. And for greater authenticity we should snare them at Stratford- upon-Avon... Two thousand. Pounds. Guineas. Dollars? *(To self.)* Which, dammit!

ALICE: My father deals with Barclay's. I'll open an account you can draw on. Now, my dear friend—let's get down to specifics. Which play? What birds?

Lights off ALICE and ARTHUR. Up on MIKE and FRANCES. MIKE has a small sack of orchids.

FRANCES: When do you start back?

MIKE: Right away.

FRANCES: Are Fric and Frac OK with everything?

MIKE: I had to stop them harvesting too many. I'll pay them as soon as we get to San Fernando. Then I'll catch the puddle jumper to Caracas, there's a morning flight to Miami—I can be in Pittsburgh by the weekend, OK? *(Pause.)* Doctor?

FRANCES: I'm here.

MIKE: Thought I'd lost you.

FRANCES: Mike, there's a small problem.

MIKE: What.

FRANCES: Money.

MIKE: You said you'd wired it!

FRANCES: I know. I lied. You were on the river already and I didn't want to worry you. I lied. I'm sorry.

MIKE has hung up. Black on him.

Mike? Mike? Mike!

Black on FRANCES. Light on ARTHUR, who is

furtively consulting Shakespeare's 'The Collected Works'.

ARTHUR: I've found the perfect bird with which to launch our experiment. It's from the romances.

Light will come up on ALICE.

"Wilt thou be gone? It is not yet near day;
It was the nightingale, and not the lark,
That pierc'd the fearful hollow of thine ear…"

Please advise by telegram if this is suitable.

Focus over to MIKE and FRANCES, on phone again.

FRANCES: Where did you go?

MIKE: I had to get out of earshot. What do you mean—no money?! You said you'd wired the proceeds

FRANCES: —You wouldn't have gone back to look for the orchid!

MIKE: I might have. On my own. But now—I've found the orchid and I've got two guys with machetes who think they're about to live on easy street!

FRANCES: My annual research grant should've come through by now. The university's holding it up

MIKE: —What about your credit cards?

FRANCES: They're maxed.

MIKE: You have no savings?

FRANCES: Not a penny.

ARTHUR is putting the 'The Collected Works' back on the shelf when ALICE replies.

ALICE: Dearest Arthur stop. 'Romeo and Juliet' stop. Nightingales are perfect stop. Warmest regards

Alice stop.

Focus back on FRANCES and MIKE.

MIKE: Sell your car!

FRANCES: I already did, last year.

MIKE: Sell some of your orchids!

FRANCES: They're not mine to sell. The university owns everything in here. Can't your church give you a loan?

MIKE: For what?!

FRANCES: Tell them you need compassionate leave.

MIKE: I won't lie to them!

FRANCES: What did you tell them about your little jaunt up the Orinoco? Did you tell them you were looking for a swamp with blind dolphins and an orchid that smells like a dead fucking cow?

MIKE: No.

FRANCES: Didn't think so. What did you say?

MIKE: *(Beat.)* I was going on a retreat.

FRANCES: So you can lie.

Focus back on ALICE and ARTHUR. ARTHUR is combing through 'The Collected Works' again.

ARTHUR: "Merry larks are ploughman's clocks." 'Love's Labours Lost'. Wouldn't that be more appropriate for your workers? I imagine you have more ploughmen in Pittsburgh than star-crossed lovers.

ALICE: Perhaps but

ARTHUR: And larks are in 'A Midsummer's Night's Dream', as well:

"Your eyes are lodestars and your tongue's sweet air
More tuneable than lark to shepherd's ear."

Larks are the perfect choice *(To himself.)* And much easier for me to snare.

Black on them. Light on MIKE and FRANCES.

MIKE: You've got to get me money.

FRANCES: I'm trying. Please believe me. I'll go to the Dean today. But Mike, please, please try and get a loan. I wouldn't ask you if there wasn't so much at stake.

MIKE: *(Pause.)* What exactly *is* at stake? Suppose you tell me that. It's an incredible flower—but it's still just an orchid.

FRANCES: Nothing is "just an orchid".

MIKE: It's beautiful, it smells worse than anything but—I need a better reason for risking my life

FRANCES: You do? OK. OK. OK Mike. You don't have to take my word on this. Where are Fric and Frac?

MIKE: Nowhere near. Why.

FRANCES: Before they get back. Get out your knife. I have a little experiment for you to try.

Black on them. Light back on ALICE.

ALICE: Arthur, Miss Frick found an edition of 'Bartlett's Birds of England' and says your lark is as dull as ditchwater. I've got a rebellion on my hands. Miss Frick says the last thing we need in America is an ugly bird from the land of ugly people. It's your fault. Next time one of our virgins tours your fair land, even a grouchy virgin, would you please, please produce a groom? Because when a Frick doesn't get a proposal, a Frick gets bitter. The Society demands a nightingale.

Light off ALICE. Light back on FRANCES.

FRANCES: *(On the phone.)* It's O'Keefe. She knows who it is. I've been phoning for the last three days. I'm Doctor Frances Alice O'Keefe and I'm calling from the O'Keefe Conservatory. On O'Keefe Avenue. How many goddamn O'Keefes do you need? I want to speak to the Dean. I can hear her snuffling in the background. Put her on, you officious little shit or I'll come down there and— She hung up on me! That is so fucking rude. OK if the mountain won't speak to Mohammed—

FRANCES is putting on her coat and is about to leave. She comes to a dead halt at the doorway. MIKE is standing there. He's dressed as a Mormon missionary: white shirt, neat hair, little name tag etc. He has no luggage with him, having left his small plant humidor by the door as he entered.

The conservatory's only open to the public on Wednesdays. Oh great, you're a Mormon. Just what I need today, a polygamist—

MIKE: Doctor Frances O'Keefe, I presume?

FRANCES: Yes—it is—Mike?—MIKE!

Light on ARTHUR and ALICE, who's reading a telegram.

ARTHUR: Dear Alice stop Your nightingales left Bristol this morning stop

ALICE: "They have their own cabin stop And butler stop Yours Arthur stop." *(Exiting.)* Oh, they'll never believe this. Miss Mellon! Miss Frick!

ALICE and ARTHUR exit. Light full back on FRANCES and MIKE. FRANCES hugs MIKE.

FRANCES: —I'm sorry about that Mormon crack. For some reason I thought you were a Baptist.

MIKE: I am, but I travel incognito. Oldest trick in the missionary book. The skies are friendlier when you travel Mormon. No one ever checks your luggage.

FRANCES: Even now?

MIKE: Yup. Every time I fly home to Florida, I take orchids—I always dress like this. They don't check nuns either but I make a more convincing Mormon.

Sound of tires on gravel outside. ALICE bursts back on and runs to doorway. FRANCES can notice her.

ALICE: *(As she passes through.)* It's the carriage from the station! They've arrived—ladies—the birds—the nightingales are here! Miss Frick! Miss Mellon! *(Exiting outside.)* They're here!

FRANCES: Where the fuck is it!?

MIKE: You swear way too much.

FRANCES: I've been having a bad life.

MIKE: It's about to get better.

FRANCES: MIKE! Where is it—

MIKE starts unbuttoning his shirt.

What the hell are you doing!

ALICE comes back on, dragging a large case.

ALICE: I can manage I can manage oh this is so exciting.

Fumbles with latches.

FRANCES: I don't know what the hell you think you're doing.

ALICE: —My hands—look—oh I'm quite—the birds aren't singing, I suppose they only do that at night, silly me, of course, *night*ingales

FRANCES: —Stop it this minute!

MIKE: Relax!

FRANCES: I want to see the orchid!

ALICE: We'll have to open this place at night, so the millworkers can hear them. *(Latches open.)*

MIKE: You don't actually think I'd be dumb enough to carry it in a basket, do you? Mr. Customs Officer, here's my illegally imported orchid.

ALICE: "The nightingale, if she should sing by day,
When every goose is cackling, would be thought
No better musician than the wren."

Oh I don't believe that. Come out of there, Mr and Mrs Nightingale. Out you come.

ALICE reaches in. Her expression changes.

Oh my—

ALICE pulls the birds out. They are dead.

Oh my word. Oh no. They're all—

FRANCES: Stop playing games!

ALICE: They're all dead!

FRANCES: Where are the orchids!

MIKE drops his shirt. There's an orchid grafted to his chest. He bursts out laughing. Black on everyone.

End of Act One.

Act Two

MIKE is standing in front of FRANCES, just as he was at the end of Act I, with his shirt open and an orchid "grafted" to him. FRANCES tears the orchid off MIKE.

MIKE: I had you.

FRANCES: Don't be ridiculous.

MIKE: You should've seen your face. I wish I had a camera.

FRANCES: You're an asshole.

MIKE: —She's thinking, "Can they really be grafted to humans?" The famous orchid professor.

FRANCES: I knew right away. This is a dimestore phalaenopsis. Airport flowershop, right? I wipe my butt with these. This is no time for jokes; where's the real one.

MIKE: *(Getting case.)* Voila.

FRANCES: How'd they travel?

MIKE: I haven't checked since I left Venezuela.

FRANCES: Is the temperature in here—

MIKE: Feels fine.

FRANCES: And the humidity?

Tapping of a telegraph key begins under. Light grows on ALICE. MIKE is unsealing case.

MIKE: They'll need fans. They were exposed to wind. Sorry about the *(Indicates chest or orchid.)*. It's another old missionary trick. Lighten things up.

FRANCES: Hurry.

MIKE opens the case; reacts.

What!

MIKE: They're all dead! Kidding! Kidding!

FRANCES: I'll kill you.

MIKE: They're tougher than we are. Relax.

Telegraph sound is loud. Light is full on ALICE.

ALICE: The birds arrived stop All dead stop

FRANCES: Let me see them. My heart, it's going nuts—

ALICE: Nightingales are too delicate stop Need new birds fast stop Frick is fractious.

ALICE exits. MIKE is pulling out an orchid now—it's a bright blue, physically gorgeous. FRANCES leans in to hold it.

FRANCES: The colour! *(Falls back at the smell.)* Jesus!

MIKE: It's exactly as Paxton wrote.

FRANCES: "The Caprisian blue belies an odour akin to rotting meat."

MIKE: My guess is that it's pollenated by flies—they're attracted to it because they think it's carrion. Betcha I can prove it. *(Pulls back a petal.)* Yup—one genuine Orinoco fly.

FRANCES: The last time I smelt anything this bad was when one of the park cats crawled under here and died.

MIKE: I was sure the flight attendants would notice. You get used to it.

FRANCES: *(Holding it happily.)* I already have.

MIKE: There's five of them.

FRANCES: Easily enough for cloning.

MIKE: Yeah.

FRANCES: Wow!

MIKE: Everything we need.

FRANCES: *(Not hearing him.)* So your church came through. That's good because I haven't got to first base here—look at it in the light

MIKE: —Everything *we* need

FRANCES: —God bless the Baptists. Do you have to pay them back or can I just mail some Bibles somewhere?

MIKE: *(Taking the flower from her.)* You're not listening to me. As soon as you told me what these do, why they're sacred—I knew I couldn't just dump them off here and go back

FRANCES: —But our contract

MIKE: —What contract?

FRANCES: Our agreement, then

MIKE: —You haven't honoured any part of it. If anyone owns these, it's the Southern Baptist Convention.

FRANCES: Don't be ridiculous.

MIKE: They "paid" to have them harvested. And, I've paid too.

FRANCES: How have you paid—you said they lent you money.

MIKE: *(Fairly matter of factly, enumerating.)* I've lied to them. I lied about my trip up the Orinoco, I lied about why I needed leave, I lied to Fric and Frac, I lied at Customs, I've lied more in the last month than in my entire life.

FRANCES: Your point?

MIKE: I'm a missionary?

FRANCES indicates she still doesn't get it.

We aren't supposed to lie?

FRANCES: Just threaten.

MIKE: I'm a missionary who loves God and orchids, in that order. I mean, I did. But with these— everything gets reversed.

FRANCES: You must've known that.

MIKE: They always win.

They admire the flowers.

FRANCES: How does a missionary man get hooked anyway?

MIKE: Like everyone else. I saw one. Just a slipper orchid. I was leading a church-school trip, we visited an orchid grower and there it was. I couldn't tear myself away. And then, when we were leaving, they gave us all seedlings, they might as well have given me crack.

FRANCES: Does anyone know you're here?

MIKE: The church thinks I'm at home, in Orlando. Resting. Another lie. Please let me stay.

FRANCES: *(Gentle.)* I can't hire you.

MIKE: I don't need to be paid.

Focus back on ALICE. Letter-writing convention.

ALICE: Dear Arthur. I apologize for yesterday's telegram.

If it sounded curt, well, blame it on the medium. Telegrams abbreviate us into rudeness. But I was upset. The birds were decomposing before our very eyes.

ARTHUR: "Miss Frick could barely contain her glee."

ALICE: She said, "Why don't we just admit we're a pack of useless spinsters and get on with it?" I lost my temper. I said, "What is this 'it' we're supposed to get on with, Miss Frick? Massacring steel-workers?"

ARTHUR: Oh, that's good

ALICE: —She left in a huff and Miss Mellon followed and then Miss Duryea and the Willett girls—down my drive they clucked. Now I'm alone. Me, and a pair of rotting nightingales.

ARTHUR: And a hundred thousand square feet of orchids.

Light off ALICE and ARTHUR. Focus back on FRANCES and MIKE. He is now taking in his surroundings and is clearly awestruck.

MIKE: I heard it was amazing but—how many square feet is this?

FRANCES: Over 200,000 now. About a quarter is mine, for the orchids.

MIKE: Who owns the rest?

FRANCES: Oh, the university owns everything. I'm here on sufferance.

MIKE: But it's the 'O'Keefe'!

FRANCES: Alice left it to the university. Up 'till now there's been some marginal P-R value in having me here—the nutty professor Victorian Christmas-type thing

MIKE: —It needs maintenance.

FRANCES: Big time.

MIKE: How big's your staff?

FRANCES indicates herself.

What!?

FRANCES: Every now and then I get a student on a scholarship but the moronic little bastards never seem to stay. It wasn't always this bad. I used to get funding. But—OK—you want the paranoid nutty professor? See that construction over there? That's going to be the Vitakampf Research Centre.

MIKE: Vitakampf.

FRANCES: Uh huh. That's where the bucks are. The day they broke ground for that place, my funding began drying up. So if you're thinking you have a future here...

MIKE: I worked every summer for Orlando Orchids.

FRANCES: That's great, none better but

MIKE: —So I've hybridized, I've cloned.

FRANCES: I can't pay you!

MIKE: I already told you—I don't want money! Anyway, "It's easier for a camel to go through the eye of a needle, than a rich man to enter the kingdom of God."

FRANCES: *(Pause.)* I could use the help.

MIKE: Yes?

FRANCES: Sometimes I get ideas and there's no one to bounce them off—

MIKE: I'm great for bouncing ideas off.

FRANCES: I'm not always even-tempered.

MIKE: I am.

FRANCES: I hate practical jokes.

MIKE: You just don't like being fooled.

FRANCES: You'll have to cut with the fucking Bible quotes.

MIKE: How badly do you need me?

FRANCES: No more than one quote a day.

MIKE: Three.

FRANCES: Two.

MIKE: Deal. And your swearing?

FRANCES: Quit trying to hybridize me.

MIKE: *(As they exit.)* What're you doing to me?

Focus off FRANCES and MIKE. Light on ALICE and ARTHUR. She is mostly in the letter-writing convention.

ALICE: Nightingales don't have the constitution to travel. But I'm not giving up on the birds of Shakespeare, oh no. And the ladies can't keep away from my orchids. Even Miss Frick. Especially Miss Frick. She swears she only likes ferns but I've caught her touching my flowers. When she thinks I'm not looking—her pointy little talons dart out and—she pushes up against them. She blushes, she says the beads of perspiration are from the heat of the greenhouse but it's not, I know it's not... They'll come back. And Arthur, when they do, I want to present them with a new option—one that won't arrive decomposed.

ALICE has brought forward a hybrid—the Phaius Grandfolius—during this and set it down. She exits. MIKE picks it up.

FRANCES: Alice's hybrids.

MIKE: The late great Alice O'Keefe. You know how many websites there are on her?

FRANCES: Don't remind me.

MIKE: They all mention the bird fiasco. There's hardly anything on her hybrids.

FRANCES: The older she was, the wilder they got. The more sexual. OK smart guy, what's this.

MIKE: Phaius Grandfolius. From Florida. It must be nearly a century old.

FRANCES: I'm impressed. Come see what I've got over here.

FRANCES leads MIKE off. ALICE and ARTHUR enter. The latter is madly combing through 'The Collected Works'.

ARTHUR: What about swans? They're in 'Othello'.

ALICE: We've already got them in America. And don't suggest gulls, we have plenty.

ARTHUR: Shakespeare didn't mean the bird when he used 'gull'—the meaning is 'to trick'.

ALICE: There's a gull in 'Timon of Athens'. When they are calling in Timon's debts:

"I do fear
when every feather sticks in his own wing
Lord Timon will be left a naked gull..."

ARTHUR: I uh yes I'd forgotten that. Do you have his entire works memorized?

ALICE: Just the flower and bird references.

ARTHUR: All of them?

ALICE: Oh, I have to confess—not the histories. Not yet.

And Arthur—no falcons. They'd be dreadfully unhappy in here. We'd have to clip their wings. That's the wrong message to be sending to the millworkers. I need a small, hardy species.

ARTHUR: I might have an idea.

ALICE: *(Aside, as she exits.)* The English sometimes do.

ALICE and ARTHUR exit. FRANCES and MIKE are working on the new orchids.

FRANCES: So let me get this straight. You were in Venezuela because of the orchids—or to convert the savages?

MIKE: They're not savages. They were already Christian.

FRANCES: Then why do they need converting?

MIKE: We weren't "converting" them. It was more like redirecting.

FRANCES: They weren't good enough Christians?

MIKE: Well—

FRANCES: You couldn't leave well enough alone?

MIKE: Why do you hybridize?

FRANCES: I hybridize—plants—because I'm curious. You convert—excuse me, "re-direct"—people—because you make assumptions about what's good for them.

MIKE: Except, they want to change. They're Catholics, and that's doing nothing for them—it just keeps them in their place; poor, uneducated, under the thumb of the priests. We teach them personal affirmation through Jesus. We've got a health clinic—which they help run. Plus at our services we've got electric guitars.

FRANCES: Ahhh.

MIKE: We're American and modern. That's what they want to be.

FRANCES: But why the Orinoco?

MIKE: When I graduated from seminary I had my choice of three mission fields: Iowa, Quebec or Venezuela. I uh kind of chose the one with the best orchids.

FRANCES: I'd have thought these refute the existence of God.

MIKE: Why?

FRANCES: I'm assuming you're a Creationist.

MIKE: A good scientist shouldn't assume anything, should she?

FRANCES: Mike, if there's ever been a plant species that proves evolution—it's the orchid. *(Runs to get the long-petaled Madagascar orchid.)* This is the one that caught Darwin's eye. It's from Madagascar.

MIKE: You have one—awesome.

FRANCES: —Of course, for this to be pollenated, in the wild, it requires an insect with a foot-long snout. And lo and behold—one had evolved.

MIKE: *(Holds up another orchid.)* But look at this—and think with your heart—and tell me there's no God.

FRANCES: That's a hybrid. I made it. So if there's a God, you're looking at her. And if I'm God—what does that make you?

MIKE: Sliding backwards, and fast.

Focus off FRANCES and MIKE. ALICE and ARTHUR again.

ALICE: Arthur, I've been thinking about the poor birds—travelling all the way from there to here, all alone. They need a chaperon. A gentleman chaperon.

ARTHUR: Do you have one in mind?

ALICE: Don't be a tease. I will wire your passage tomorrow. Oh Arthur: what will you bring me?

ARTHUR: Wouldn't you rather have a surprise?

ALICE: No.

ARTHUR: Well a surprise is what you'll get.

ALICE and ARTHUR exit. Focus back on MIKE and FRANCES.

FRANCES: What'll we call it?

MIKE: The Mike?

FRANCES: Maybe we should name it after Paxton.

MIKE: Or your aunt? She's the one who kept the journal safe.

FRANCES: And she's the one with the shaky reputation. OK. 'Aliciana' it is. *(Pause.)* Did you try it?

MIKE: Yes.

FRANCES: *(Pause.)* Did it work?

MIKE: See for yourself.

FRANCES: You're not serious—

MIKE: Come on—

FRANCES: You do it.

MIKE: But I already know.

FRANCES: Men before ladies. Alice would insist.

MIKE: There's no etiquette for self-mutilation. Why doctor, I don't think you believe!

FRANCES: I believe.

MIKE: Liar.

FRANCES: I so totally believe, I don't need a demonstration. You know, for a Christian, you're awfully hung up on evidence.

MIKE: For a scientist, you're awful chicken. Come on.

FRANCES: *(Takes knife.)* It's unnatural.

MIKE: Unnatural can be good.

FRANCES: Spoken like a true Baptist. Just a nick.

FRANCES hands knife back to MIKE.

You'll have to cut me.

MIKE: Now that's unnatural.

FRANCES: Hurry up.

MIKE: Isn't this against some university code of conduct?

FRANCES: Mike!

MIKE: What if the Dean walks in?

FRANCES: She could never find this place. That's half the problem. Now cut me.

MIKE cuts FRANCES's arm. A thin red line appears. FRANCES wobbles a bit.

MIKE: Too much? Sorry—sorry -

FRANCES: It's OK. Whoah -

MIKE: Frances?

FRANCES: I'm fine. It's like the time I flew. I just feel a bit woozy—

MIKE: Hold your arm out—

MIKE takes a bit of the orchid petal and squeezes it.

Watch. One drop.

MIKE rubs his fingers over FRANCES's cut.

You should have looked.

FRANCES: I can't.

MIKE: You missed the show.

FRANCES: I hate blood.

MIKE: What blood?

FRANCES: *(Looks.)* Jesus Murphy!

MIKE: You can't even see the nick. There's no danger of infection, either—I could've made the incision with a rusty nail.

FRANCES: It's exactly as Paxton wrote! He wasn't delusional! Not that I ever doubted! Let's do you! I can watch that.

MIKE: OK, where.

FRANCES: You decide.

MIKE: My heart.

FRANCES: Really?

MIKE pulls back his shirt and FRANCES makes a small cut across his heart. She then rubs the orchid over it—and the bleeding instantly disappears. They are both a bit giddy.

My turn again.

MIKE pulls back FRANCES's shirt, and is about to nick her collarbone.

Do it somewhere where I can see.

Focus moves to ALICE and ARTHUR. Under their

scene, MIKE pulls back FRANCES's shirt and nicks her upper arm. He clears the bleeding with the plant and then turns his cheek. FRANCES cuts him and clears it. She holds out her palms to him. He pulls them to him and begins cutting. Meanwhile, ALICE has returned and is tending to an orchid. There is a rapping sound. ARTHUR enters and sees ALICE.

ARTHUR: Alice O'Keefe, I presume?

ALICE: Arthur? Arthur!

ALICE seems about to throw her arms around ARTHUR, but instead grasps and shakes his hand.

Welcome! I'm sorry—I was working on my flowers—I had meant to wait for you on the drive—I didn't hear a carriage!

ARTHUR: I walked from the station.

ALICE: But that's two miles! Oh—my manners—

ALICE pumps ARTHUR's hand again.

Welcome to America! You must be exhausted!

ALICE does not let go of ARTHUR's hand, but rather begins to examine it.

ARTHUR: On the contrary, dear Alice. I'm exhilarated. I'm sorry—is there something wrong—

ALICE: Your hands.

ARTHUR: Yes?

ALICE: They're—oh—forgive me

ARTHUR: *(With her.)* —One, two, left, right. *(Then.)* Oh, the callouses? These are from mucking about with my orchids. If the boys aren't working fast enough, I jump right in.

ALICE is staring at his face.

Is there something wrong with my face, too?

ALICE: No!

ARTHUR: But you're staring.

ALICE: It's your age.

ARTHUR: Too old, too young, too

ALICE begins shaking ARTHUR's hand again.

ALICE: —You're much younger than I expected. We never discussed your age in your letters. It's the English accent. An accent always makes a man seem ancient. Not that I've actually heard your accent until now but when I read your letters I felt I could hear it and I thought you'd be at least fifty oh listen to me -

Cellphone starts, off.

ARTHUR: *(Aging.)* I could act older for you.

ALICE: You're fine as you are. It's very nice you're younger than I anticipated.

ARTHUR: And if you'll forgive me—you're much, much younger than I'd expected.

ALICE: 29.

ARTHUR: But in your letters—

ALICE: 29 in American years. Now come—let me get you a cup of tea. *(Exiting.)* Or perhaps you'd prefer something stronger.

ALICE and ARTHUR have exited. The sound of the phone ringing continues.

FRANCES: Where is the damn thing!?

MIKE: *(Holding her cell out to her.)* Someone wants you awful bad.

FRANCES: *(Answering.)* O'Keefe. Who's this? *(Cups phone; makes a face.)* The campus paper. *(Back to phone.)* Yes? What? *(Listens with increasing distress; MIKE registers.)* Where'd you hear that? The Dean's office? They sent out a fax—no, I haven't looked. I'll get back to you. *(Hangs up.)* Fucking hell. I don't believe it. I don't fucking believe it.

MIKE: What!

FRANCES: *(Exiting.)* I've got to check the fax machine—

FRANCES exits. MIKE stays. ARTHUR and ALICE return.

ARTHUR: How else did you imagine me?

ALICE: Perhaps obese. Because of all the exotic animals you eat. Cassowary, python—they must be fattening. And your double-barrelled last name, well, I thought you'd look more aristocratic. No—that's a compliment! Miss Frick has met your aristocrats and she says she's never seen a homelier bunch. That's rude too. I'm not doing well. Should we lie down? I mean, you must be tired. I go to bed for a day if I so much as take a carriage downtown, did I tell you about the time I took the train to Latrobe I puked for a week—yes I did, I tell everyone, lord, listen to me prattle. You say something.

ARTHUR: Dear, dear Alice. Thank you for luring me to this glorious land. There is so much energy here. As I walked from the station—I just felt over-full. It was as if I'd eaten an entire kangaroo.

ALICE: Yes, we do have that effect on people.

ARTHUR has begun to breathe deeply. ALICE watches with increasing concern.

Are you—is everything alright?

ARTHUR: Just smell this energy! This virility! This brashness!

ALICE sniffs doubtfully.

This glorious American air!

ARTHUR flings open the conservatory door, takes a deep breath, and chokes.

ALICE: That's the glorious Homestead Mill. It's our civic cross. It's like living under a smoking mattress.

ARTHUR: It's rather like London.

ALICE: Miss Frick says it's worse. She says that should make us proud. She sees the air as a tangible measure of our prosperity. Certainly, it's a measure of hers.

ARTHUR: I believe she's correct. It is a stronger smog. Potent. Potent American soot. Where is Miss Frick?

ALICE: She'll be here tomorrow. Come.

ALICE is going outside to the drive. ARTHUR follows.

Your luggage should have arrived by now.

ALICE has almost exited.

Our luggage.

ALICE and ARTHUR exit. FRANCES returns, holding a fax.

FRANCES: I'm sorry Mike. We were having so much fun mutilating each other—and then I get that call. The campus paper—they were following up on a fax.

MIKE: About the orchid? How'd they hear

FRANCES: —No, about this place.

MIKE: What about it?

FRANCES: *(Holds up fax.)* The university's shutting us down.

FRANCES and MIKE exit. ARTHUR hurries back on, coughing a bit. ALICE follows.

ALICE: If I'd known exactly when you were arriving I'd have arranged for the wind to blow west.

ARTHUR: You're very charming.

ALICE: I am? I could at least have had the carriage waiting for you. I don't know why your trunks haven't arrived yet—you hired a wagon for them I assume

ARTHUR: —I uh

ALICE: —Of course, you stored them at the station. Very wise. Oh Arthur, it's wonderful, really wonderful to meet you at last. Imagine thinking you'd be seventy and bulbous! Miss Frick'll require proof of identity. Some official document flaunting your stately surname.

ARTHUR: That may be hard to supply.

ALICE: Oh?

ARTHUR: I'm not quite the man you think I am.

ALICE: Pardon?

ARTHUR: I'm not Arthur Fox-Timlin.

Focus off ALICE and ARTHUR. FRANCES returns, followed by MIKE. She is struggling with her winter coat.

FRANCES: It wouldn't occur to them to warn me. And you should hear the university doublespeak: "Restructuring and rationalization". The two R's. *(Reading.)* "Part of the ongoing consolidation of the university's biotech research." Everything is to be located in that new monstrosity—

MIKE: Vitakampf—

FRANCES: The university's biggest donor. You know what's ironic? The O'Keefe family used to be the university's biggest donor. And we didn't go around purging faculty. Come on Mike, grab a coat. Time to visit the Dean. Bring the orchid.

FRANCES and MIKE exit.

ALICE: What do you mean, you're not Arthur Fox-Timlin?

ARTHUR: It happened at Ellis Island.

ALICE: What happened at—you went through Ellis?

ARTHUR: Yes, the Americans all disembarked at Manhattan but we

ALICE: —You shouldn't have had to go through Ellis

ARTHUR: —Oh, but I'm glad I did! Of course I was impatient to get off but I said to myself, "Arthur, savour this moment! A glorious adventure has begun." I listened intently to the voices around me—the customs officers, the negro porters—all of them so, so...

ALICE: American?

ARTHUR: So richly American. So intoxicating!

ALICE: We must bottle and sell this!

ARTHUR: Now you're teasing me.

ALICE: It's terrible you had to go through Ellis.

ARTHUR: My head was swimming. It was like the time I ate fried anteater! I approached the counter. I seized the clerk's hand and shook it. Oh, he was a fine man, a big-boned chap with a majestic great paw. I'm sure this fellow grew up on—on an Ohio farm—mingling his sweat with the virgin soil as he shucked hay.

ALICE: I'm not completely sure hay gets shucked.

ARTHUR: Corn?

ALICE: Sure.

ARTHUR: I shook his hand vigorously. "I am tickled pink to be here," I said.

He replied, with utter simplicity. "Where are you coming from?"

"Never mind where I'm coming from," I said. "It's where I'm headed that really matters. And you, sir, you are my first American on American soil. You must tell me your name."

He paused. "Calvert," he said. "William Washington Calvert."

William Washington Calvert! Oh, I was filled with such unreserved joy—what a splendid name for one's first American! And then, with that same utter simplicity, Mr. William Washington Calvert asked me my name, saying he had to write it in his ledger. The Great Ledger of America.

"Arthur," I started. "Christian name, Arthur." And then do you know what I did, dear, dear Alice? Can you ever guess what I did at that precise moment in time?

ALICE: Do I dare?

ARTHUR: I killed Timlin.

Light off ALICE and ARTHUR. FRANCES is standing in Dean Fulton's office, a tight light on her. MIKE is standing behind her.

FRANCES: Well well well. We finally meet. I was beginning to think you were an imaginary bureaucrat, just a paper-pushing hallucination—but here you are...

Now you listen to me, Dean Fulton. First of all. In the future, when I phone your office, let me make this clear: I will not tolerate being redirected to the University Public Relations Department. Anyway, why the fuck does a university need public relations? The pursuit of knowledge shouldn't require public relations—

SIT BACK DOWN! Now: I am popular in this city; the public knows and loves me from my Victorian Christmas and my Elvis Valentines— PUT THAT PHONE DOWN! Yes I know what my employment contract says, and I know what the lease on the conservatory says and—

An alarm will begin ringing, in the distance.

ALL RIGHT! Just tell me this one thing. Who really wants me out? It's not you. You've been Dean for ten years and you've never set foot in the place. I doubt you even understand what I'm researching. As I recall, your background is Restoration Comedy. Whatever the fuck that is. So who's telling you to shut me down? You don't want to answer? Mike?

MIKE steps forward. Under, sound of sirens start.

This is my assistant. He won't hurt you. He's a Baptist I rescued from the South American rain forest.

Sirens in distance draw closer.

Dean. I'm about to show you something you'll never see in one of your silly comedies. Knife please.

MIKE hands FRANCES the knife and she cuts MIKE.

Orchid.

MIKE hands FRANCES the orchid and she clears his wound.

Betcha Vitakampf can't do that. Now, Dean Fulton: hold out your arm…

Holding the knife, FRANCES and MIKE advance on the Dean. Black on them; light on ALICE and ARTHUR.

ALICE: You killed Timlin?

ARTHUR: Gone, dead, zoop!

ALICE: Zoop?

ARTHUR: Erased.

ALICE: And the lovely hyphen?

ARTHUR: Also gone. Hyphen and Timlin, zoop zoop. A thousand years of English pretension erased in one Ohio penstroke.

ALICE: When you go back, will you revert?

ARTHUR: I'm not going back

ALICE: —Because surely the double barrel must be an advantage there—did you just say—

ARTHUR: I'm casting my lot in with William Washington Calvert and the poor late Stanley Bluebird and the charming Miss Frick—and Alice O'Keefe.

ALICE: I uh we're honoured. Tru-ly.

ARTHUR: Good.

ALICE: But I'm starting to get worried about your luggage. I'll send a carriage down for it—and the birds. You haven't even mentioned them.

ARTHUR: Oh yes, the birds. That's another story. Oh Alice, dearest of all Alices. I'm rather afraid there is no luggage. Not at the station. No luggage. No birds.

Focus off ALICE and ARTHUR. Light on a very dejected MIKE and FRANCES, returning to the conservatory.

FRANCES: I still say calling the campus security was over-reacting.

MIKE: The knife made her oddly nervous.

FRANCES: As if I'd actually slash her.

MIKE: You slashed me.

FRANCES: And I healed you, too. For a man of God, you threw that cop an impressive left hook.

MIKE: I was afraid he was going to squash the flower. D'you think the Dean'll press charges?

FRANCES: If she thinks it'll get rid of me faster, yup.

MIKE: How much time will it take

FRANCES: —Two years before we can have enough plants cloned for the clinical trials

MIKE: —For them to kick us out.

FRANCES: Oh. Normally the university moves at a snail's pace on these things. There are professors who've been dead for three decades who still have offices. They call it tenure. But I've got no lease on the Conservatory. It never occurred to me to ask for one. It's the O'Keefe, I'm an O'Keefe

MIKE: —So it could be soon.

FRANCES: I just gave them all the eviction ammo they need. And you know what's ironic? After our little demo back there, I bet they're finally starting to believe in my orchid.

MIKE: Dean Fulton.

FRANCES: The Dean and her donors. The ones calling the shots. *(Exiting.)* The ones controlling research around here. You don't give the university fifty million without getting something back.

FRANCES holds up the orchid. FRANCES and MIKE exit. Light back on ALICE and ARTHUR.

ALICE: If the birds aren't here, and they aren't at the station—where are they?

ARTHUR: New York.

ALICE: What?

ARTHUR: Customs Shed 17. Ellis Island. They've been distrained.

ALICE: Why?!

ARTHUR: There was a small misunderstanding.

ALICE: Is that where your belongings are, too?

ARTHUR: There were some difficulties with my passage.

ALICE: Apparently.

ARTHUR: I had enough money to get on the ship but perhaps not quite enough to get off.

ALICE: But I wired you two thousand dollars!

ARTHUR: Yes but

ALICE: —Surely someone could have vouched for you on board—with your connections. Oh Arthur, I'm completely baffled by this.

ARTHUR: The collecting of the birds was more expensive than anticipated.

ALICE: I would have sent you more!

ARTHUR: And I uh had debts—from the Acclimatization Society

ALICE: —Arthur

ARTHUR: —And so my money…

ALICE: Zoop?

ARTHUR: Yes. Somewhat.

ALICE: Well don't I just have the knack. Who'd have thought it would be so darn difficult to bring a few birds to America. First I get two dead nightingales. Then I get a whole case of live birds, but in the wrong city. Plus an Englishman who since coming to America has lost half his name and all his fortune.

ARTHUR: I'm dreadfully sorry.

ALICE: Tell that to Miss Frick! Tell her you're sorry our birds are distrained! How much will it cost me to spring them from Customs Shed 17?

ARTHUR: Two thousand.

ALICE: That's tidy. Arthur. I have one more question and I want an honest answer. Far better to be honest with me now than have me humiliated later. Are the birds alive?

ARTHUR: Oh, very much so.

ALICE: I suppose I can wire my father's attorney in New York. With luck, we can get the birds on the overnight train—they could still get here before the Acclimatizers do, tomorrow.

ARTHUR is entranced by the orchids.

If you have no money you can hardly stay at a hotel.

ARTHUR: Oh, I can bed down here, I'm used to it.

ALICE: That would be inappropriate. I'll get you a room at

the Franklin. You don't have a change of clothes—you appear to be my brother's size—I'll send a couple of his suits down. You must look presentable tomorrow. Lord, what if the birds don't arrive by then—I'll go wire the lawyer now. *(About to leave.)* Be back here tomorrow. By 10 a.m. Mr. Fox. We'll mount vigil for the birds. The hotel is back down the hill—you'll enjoy the stroll. It's intoxicating.

ALICE storms out. ARTHUR is alone and gives himself over to the beauty of ALICE's orchids. He begins taking stock of them and produces Paxton's journal from his jacket. He consults it as he walks about. He is particularly amazed by one orchid—perhaps the Phaius Grandfolius—and he sets down Paxton's journal and picks up the flower.

ARTHUR: Oh my God…

ARTHUR sits with the orchid, and goes into full orchidelirium. MIKE and FRANCES enter. She is holding a paper.

FRANCES: They're playing hardball—it's the eviction notice.

MIKE: For when.

FRANCES: Tomorrow morning, 9 a.m. *(Pulls out phone.)*

MIKE: Who're you calling?

FRANCES: The press.

MIKE: *(Takes phone from her.)* It won't work. Don't forget—the university's got their public relations department. They'll make you out to be a nutty professor, a violent nutty professor—

ARTHUR: *(Under.)* What's this?

FRANCES: What do we do then?

MIKE: I don't know. Why do I have to think of something!

FRANCES: You're my assistant!

MIKE: I've been here one day!

FRANCES: We've been e-mailing for over a year. That's the longest professional relationship of my career. *(Pause.)* And I don't know how to win this.

MIKE: OK OK.

FRANCES: So think of something.

MIKE: *(Beat.)* Let's look at this rationally.

FRANCES: Rationally?! They're taking my orchids!

They both look at the blue orchids. Light fades on them and up again on ARTHUR, who is still with the orchid that has entranced him.

ALICE: *(Off.)* Arthur? Arthur!! Are you still there?!

ARTHUR comes to, puts the orchid down and rushes off.

ARTHUR: (Exiting.) Damn—

ALICE: *(Coming on.)* I've been horribly rude. I was just so disappointed not to have the birds and I'm sure you must be just as upset—*(She sees Paxton's journal, which he left behind.)* Oh. He's left his—*(Picks it up and runs to the door.)* Arthur? Arthur! *(Returns.)*

ALICE sits down on the bench ARTHUR just vacated and starts reading Paxton's journal. FRANCES and MIKE are with the blue orchids.

FRANCES: Put these in a humidor and take them to my apartment.

MIKE: No—they're expecting you to steal them. They'd love you to steal them. So they can catch you and totally discredit you

FRANCES: —Then let's hide them with the other orchids and come back for them in a month.

MIKE: With their smell? You can't hide these.

FRANCES: Then you'll have to take them. We can get some money out of the gift shop till—you could—you can take the bus to Florida, we can keep them at Orlando Orchids until we figure out something

MIKE: —A commercial grower won't touch these, not with a ten foot pole. Not only are they stolen from here—they're illegally imported. They could lose their licence. Anyway—I bet they've got campus security sitting out there

FRANCES: —Well, by God, no one else is getting their hands on these. Especially not Vitakampf. Let's just get the hell out of here with these—we'll figure out a plan when we're on the road.

MIKE: We won't make it out of the state.

FRANCES: What are we going to do?

ALICE: *(Reading, and realizing what's in the journal.)* "It took us twelve weeks to make our way up the Orinoco by steamer. It broke down repeatedly—if the boiler wasn't dying, then we were foundering on a rock or log. *(Going under, into transition to the morning.)*

The river was impassible above San Fernando, so we transferred to canoe, and we paddled further upstream..."

Light change. FRANCES and MIKE remain. ALICE has also remained, having spent the entire night reading the journal. ARTHUR enters, in an ill-fitting suit, and immediately begins looking for the journal. ALICE is waiting for him.

ARTHUR: Good morning.

ALICE: How did you find your rooms?

ARTHUR: Very comfortable, thank you. Oh Alice—

ALICE: And my brother's suit?

ARTHUR: A perfect fit. Alice, please, please allow me to convey my deepest apologies—

ALICE: We'll get to that—

ARTHUR: I have abused your trust. But I was so embarrassed; my impecuniosity…

ALICE: Did you steal that word, too?

ARTHUR: Beg pardon?

ALICE holds up journal.

Oh thank goodness, you found my journal. I was worried sick about it—I feared I dropped it.

ALICE holds it away from ARTHUR.

ALICE: The birds are apparently fine. They're on a train here, first class coach. Singing up a storm, I'm told.

ARTHUR: Yes, there are a dozen pairs and

ALICE: —And the money is really no great hurdle. Daddy only needs to sell a few more stoves. *(Holds journal up.)* But this is another matter. You see, I'm really just a snoopy spinster after all—I began reading "your" journal. And something immediately struck me. This is not in the same handwriting as your letters. The sentence construction, the spelling even—they're different too.

ARTHUR: I can explain

ALICE: —So I wired Paxton early this morning. At Kew.

ARTHUR: Oh.

ALICE: He has his own telegraph office! How convenient! I thought I'd ask him about my Mr. Fox. *(Produces telegram.)* Shall I read his reply? "Keep the greasy little wretch in America. But I demand the return of my journal!"

ARTHUR: I don't know what he's talking about.

ALICE: Oh, I think you do. This is Paxton's journal, not yours. The technical instructions, his searches for orchids—there's an utterly amazing account of his recent trip up the Orinoco... How could this belong to anyone else? How could it be yours? You stole this. Well? You could at least have the good grace to look ashamed.

ARTHUR: *(Indicates orchids.)* And these?

ALICE: What!

ARTHUR: These weren't stolen?

ALICE: I paid for every last orchid in here!

ARTHUR: You paid the thieves.

ALICE: That's absurd.

ARTHUR: How do you think we built the collection at Kew?

ALICE: I've never dealt with a thief in my life. Present company excluded. Now. Arthur.The ladies of the Acclimatization Society of America will be here in an hour, to await the birds' arrival. Before that I need to have everything straight in my mind. I need to know the truth—so I can tell better lies.

Focus off ALICE and ARTHUR. Noises have started offstage—car doors etc. FRANCES and MIKE return.

FRANCES: *(Going to the window.)* Just as I thought, there they are. Campus security. Mike? I never thought I'd say this. From the bottom of my heart, I wish that was a busload of Shriners.

Focus back on ARTHUR and ALICE.

ALICE: Let's start with this: who are you?

ARTHUR: I was an employee at Kew.

ALICE: Not Paxton's chum.

ARTHUR: I worked with his orchids.

ALICE: Which explains your hands.

ARTHUR: And sometimes, if he needed help at a banquet. At an Acclimatization dinner—

ALICE: Which is how you knew all their business.

ARTHUR: Yes.

ALICE: You never ate zebra?

ARTHUR: Oh yes! We tasted everything—in the kitchen.

ALICE: That's good, because the ladies will ask. How did you get my letter?

ARTHUR: Sir Joseph was away and there was a mound of unopened letters on his desk.

ALICE: Why were you hovering about his office?

ARTHUR: His orchids—I was tending to them. I saw your letter, with its American stamp—and I took it.

ALICE: Stealing mail is a federal offence.

ARTHUR: I didn't steal it in America!

ALICE: It's legal in England?

ARTHUR: I've never done anything like this, Alice, Miss O'Keefe, you have to believe me! I've worked at

Kew since I was twelve, my record was blameless but—when I saw your letter, I—I recognized your handwriting. You had written before—it was me who packed you that first cattleya. I thought I would—I could send you some more orchids…I wanted someone to correspond with.

ALICE: Why not just write me as yourself? I have a dozen penpals all over the world.

ARTHUR: None like me, I wager. I'm the Second Under Gardener. As far as Sir is concerned, I'll always be the one at the boring end of the shovel.

ALICE: But we share our love of orchids and—hopefully—birds

ARTHUR: —And dammit—excuse me—but that's the frustrating thing! I know my orchids! I have worked at the side of the greatest. Yes, I cleaned his pots and did his shovelling but he talked to me, he told me things

ALICE: —Then why steal his journal?

ARTHUR: Oh Ma'am—you said you read it.

ALICE: I was up all night.

ARTHUR: Then you must understand.

ALICE: Of course I understand, Arthur. If I'd been in your shoes—I'd have stolen it too.

ALICE and ARTHUR remain. There is banging on the door as focus is restored to FRANCES and MIKE. MIKE heads to the window with the orchids.

FRANCES: What're you doing!? It's freezing out there!

MIKE: We have to kill them. It's the only way to keep them from Vitakampf.

FRANCES: Do you really think they care about them? I'd give

you odds that they want nothing to do with these—what—a public domain flower that any orchid grower could clone—an orchid that does the same things as the drugs they're developing? They don't want the competition!

MIKE: Perhaps. But after our demonstration with the Dean, I don't know. Maybe they'll lock these away—maybe they'll use them. Neither alternative is any good. Do you agree? So then let's get rid of this batch. Don't forget, we're the only two who know where the rest are. We can put them on the open market, free for all

FRANCES: *(Beat.)* Wait. Mike. Wait.

MIKE: What.

FRANCES: Go stall them.

MIKE: What!

FRANCES: This is something I should do. Go!

MIKE hesitates.

Go!

There is more banging off, and this pulls MIKE away. He exits. His following lines will be spoken off, intermittently and under the others, not highly audible.

MIKE: *(Off, under the following speeches.)* Doctor O'Keefe? I don't know if she's still here. I'll have to check. No—you wait there please. I'll go find her. You sure she wasn't in the rose arbor? Did you look at the far end—she might be in the shed—I'll try the lilies. Sometimes she's in the lilies. You look down there.

FRANCES picks up the orchids and begins walking towards the window, but comes to a stop when she reaches ALICE and ARTHUR.

ALICE: Did you know there are orchids that change colour depending on their locale? If they're in shade, they actually get brighter!

ARTHUR: Of course.

ALICE: Well, you had me fooled. I believed you were Paxton's colleague. But then, I'm a gullible spinster. Arthur: can you fool a Frick?

ARTHUR: I uh I can try.

ALICE: You'll do better than "try". Fox is your real name?

ARTHUR: Yes.

ALICE: Where did Timlin come from?

ARTHUR: The Kew Gardens chaplain. It sounded—educated.

ALICE: Please tell me there was a William Washington Calvert.

ARTHUR: Oh yes, that was all true—

ALICE: I think the ladies might enjoy that story. *(Points to an orchid.)* What's this.

FRANCES & ARTHUR: Miltonia reozlii.

ARTHUR: A good specimen, too.

ALICE: And that?

FRANCES & ARTHUR: A Parishii.

FRANCES: One of your favourites

ALICE: —It's my favourite. And this?

ARTHUR: You're testing my memory.

FRANCES: It's the cattleya Sir Joseph sent you.

ARTHUR: Has something been nibbling on it?

ALICE: The late Stanley.

ARTHUR: *(Enjoying the test.)* Oncidium papilio.

FRANCES: *(Also having fun.)* Phalaenopsis Renanthera Vanda.

ALICE: And you honestly know how to hybridize?

FRANCES: Of course

ARTHUR: —Oh yes. I just hybridized a dowiana and a boothiana. That is, Paxton did. I watched. His notes are in the journal.

ALICE: Could you hybridize one for me?

FRANCES: Get him to teach you

ARTHUR: —I can teach you.

ALICE: Oh. *(Pause.)* Arthur—the birds—in addition to being alive—they are truly from Shakespeare?

ARTHUR: 'Henry IV'.

ALICE: Which part.

ARTHUR: One.

ALICE: Leave the rest a surprise. It'll be a refreshing change to get a good one.

FRANCES: Famous last words.

ALICE: I must send word to father. I'm rather afraid he wants you horsewhipped. *(Looks out the window.)* Oh lord, the ladies are marching up the drive! Arthur—it no longer matters who you were. It's what I want you to be that is important now. Send your accent skyward. Zoop. Charm the pants off them—that's an American expression, don't take it literally.

ARTHUR: Then you're not sending me back?

ALICE: Of course not. With your knowledge and Paxton's journal I'm going to have the best damn orchids in America. *(Looks out window again.)* There's the carriage with the birds. Perfect timing. Arthur—

ALICE and ARTHUR exit. MIKE runs in past them.

MIKE: They've got a warrant for your arrest—attempted assault. I sent them off into the roses—Frances? You've got to get rid of them.

FRANCES: I know.

MIKE: Now!

FRANCES: Stall them. Just another minute. Mike—this is the last time I'll be here. They'll never let me back. Please.

MIKE exits. ALICE and ARTHUR burst back in, hauling the crate of birds. FRANCES watches from slightly off.

ALICE: Ladies, welcome to the moment of truth. First—allow me to present, direct from his bosom buddy Sir Joseph Paxton's conservatory at Kew—Mr. Arthur Fox.

A smattering of applause—gloved hands. ARTHUR acknowledges it gracefully.

Present the crate. Please.

ARTHUR pulls it out. There are faint sounds from its interior.

I can hear this group. Thank goodness for that. Will you do the honours then, Mr. Fox?

ARTHUR: It would be my pleasure, Miss O'Keefe.

ALICE: *(To ladies.)* Don't you just love his accent?

ARTHUR: Ladies, when our last experiment failed, I realized we needed a hardier, more adaptable species than the nightingale. And I immediately thought of this one, from 'Henry IV'.

ALICE: Part One.

ARTHUR: You'll find this species an excellent mimic. In Shakespearean times, people would keep them in cages, like some do today with budgerigars.

ALICE: Budgerigars.

ALICE: These birds can whistle, and even imitate a man's voice. So in 'Henry IV', when Hotspur wanted to vex Bolingbroke—you'll recall of course that Bolingbroke's mortal enemy was Mortimer—Hotspur said:

"But I will find him when he lies asleep,
And in his ear I'll holla "Mortimer!"
Nay, I'll have a *(Indicates crated birds.)* shall be taught to speak
Nothing but "Mortimer" and give it to him
To keep his anger still in motion."

ALICE: Your command of Shakespeare is inspiring. You must give a lecture. Not now. Keep at it.

ARTHUR: Then-here-goes!

FRANCES and ALICE both rush over to look in the crate. As ARTHUR pulls back the lid, the raucous sound of starlings fills the room. The light goes tight on ALICE and FRANCES.

ALICE: Starlings!

FRANCES: The ugliest fucking bird in Shakespeare. And the most prolific.

ALICE: Look—they've begun laying eggs.

ALICE turns to FRANCES.

They'll never stop laughing at me.

FRANCES: I know.

ALICE: Never. The books—they'll all blame me. They'll make me out to be a dilettante. They'll forget that I built this and grew these...because I brought starlings to America. A billion horrible starlings.

ALICE turns back to ARTHUR. She and ARTHUR are avoiding the swooping birds.

The ladies couldn't get out of here fast enough!

ARTHUR: I'm sorry—I thought they were—they're very hardy

ALICE: —They're just so ugly! So disgusting! The birds of Shakespeare—we wanted nightingales, cuckoos—

ALICE has gone to the window. She now opens it. Some snow drifts in. FRANCES hurries over with her, carrying the blue orchids. They have left Paxton's journal behind.

ARTHUR: What are you doing!

ALICE begins scooping up the birds and directing them through the window. FRANCES is throwing out the orchids, as well.

ALICE: Fly away now! Fly! Acclimatize—or die!

FRANCES: *(With her, under.)* Die! Die!

The sound of birds rises, and segues to jungle sounds. The lighting also changes to jungle. ALICE exits with ARTHUR. MIKE and FRANCES are in a canoe.

FRANCES: Planes, cars, trains, canoes... Christ Mike, can't you stop it rocking.

MIKE: We're nearly there.

FRANCES: Have I got Alice's genes or what.

MIKE: Just have a few more yards through this, and then you'll see

FRANCES: —And tell Fric and Frac to lay off the hymns

MIKE: Just a bit of lake and then—look—

Light is up a bit more.

Frances—look.

They can see the cliff.

FRANCES: Oh my God.

MIKE: Just as Paxton promised.

FRANCES: A miniature Table Mountain.

MIKE: Yeah.

FRANCES: "As if I'd awoken from a fevered dream." But Mike—Mike? Where's the—I thought there was—shouldn't there be vegetation?

MIKE: It almost looks like

FRANCES: —It's been burned. The cliff's been burned!

MIKE: I'll go ask the boys.

MIKE exits. There is a bang, offstage. ARTHUR enters with a rifle.

ALICE: *(Pointing.)* Arthur! Over there. In the oak by the gates. Top branch.

ARTHUR enters, taking aim.

And in the maple.

ARTHUR exits again, with gun.

(To FRANCES.) Miss Frick says they've been seen as far as Boston.

There's another blast, offstage.

FRANCES: Our orchids are gone.

ALICE: Still, it would be nice not to have any reminders, here.

FRANCES: Someone wiped them out.

ALICE: We'll clear the park of them and I'll stay here

FRANCES: —They've destroyed an entire species

ALICE: —Just me and my orchids

FRANCES: Vitakampf.

ALICE: Arthur and I

FRANCES: —Of course, it was them. They stood to lose millions, billions, if that orchid ever got to market in competition with their drugs

ALICE: —We'll never leave

MIKE comes back.

FRANCES: Mike? What—why are you smiling?

MIKE: Something the boys just said.

FRANCES: The little arsonists.

MIKE: Oh Doc, I wouldn't be too hard on them. They've got their redeeming qualities.

FRANCES: Are you out of your mind?!

MIKE: They don't understand why we're so upset about the orchids they burned.

FRANCES: Let me at them, I'll make them understand

MIKE: —Because Frances, no wait, Frances—

FRANCES: What.

MIKE: Get this. Apparently there's something far, far more interesting growing just on the other side.

FRANCES: *(Stopped dead.)* On the other side—

MIKE: Of the cliff.

FRANCES: Really?

MIKE: That's the story.

FRANCES: And when you say "interesting"

MIKE: —Yeah?

FRANCES: By interesting—we're talking—orchids?

MIKE: Is there anything else?

FRANCES: No. No Mike. No there isn't. There's nothing else.

Light fades on MIKE and FRANCES.

Black.

The End.